SURVIVING PARENTAL LOSS AND GRIEF

Christian Counseling for the Grieving Heart Through Word Therapy

Dr. Theresa A. Brown

By: **Dr. Theresa A. Brown**
Created and Published by: **Jabez Publishing House, Remnant Books**
Designed by: **City of Jabez**

Copyright Disclaimer

U.S. Library of Congress Registration 1-7086955351

This book or parts thereof may not be reproduced in any form, stored in a retrieval system, or transmitted in any form by any means— electronic, mechanical, photocopy, recorded, or otherwise—without prior written permission of the publisher, except as provided by the United States of America copyright law. Biblical Reference Unless otherwise noted, scripture references were taken from the King James Version of the Holy Bible.

Copyright 2019© by Dr. Theresa A. Brown.
All Rights Reserved.

TABLE OF CONTENT

DEDICATION 4

PREFACE 5

INTRODUCTION 9

CHAPTER 1 Find Strength in Adversity 11

CHAPTER 2 Bereavement and Comfort 17

CHAPTER 3 Family Matters 23

CHAPTER 4 Christian Grief and Christian Word Therapy 29

CHAPTER 5 Childlike Faith 33

CHAPTER 6 Words Matter 39

CHAPTER 7 Choice of Words Wisely 45

CHAPTER 8 Healing Words 53

CHAPTER 9 The Five Phases of Grief 63

CHAPTER 10 Word Therapy Tool Kit 83

DEDICATION

This book is dedicated in memory of Eduardo.

PREFACE

To love is loving someone more than you love life itself. To lose a child is a love lost and something that you never get over.

Like most of the individual seek counsel in dealing with parental grief, I too have loved and lost a child. Not in infancy or adolescence but, an adult child. Age does not matter. To be perfectly honest my psychological response to the accidental death of my son, and the events which followed lead to my feeling out of control — because I was very much out of control. I couldn't change what had happened, I could not rewind to the day before. I did not know if I would ever stop hurting or if I would ever stop crying. I was physically drained from the inside out. There were times when I had no tears, and it felt like I was in a trance. I could not council myself to healing.

Of all the emotions, and visibly physical changes including weight loss, the most difficult was a broken spirt. I never stop loving God, I never blamed God, I just could not talk to God any more through prayer. It was not until I was asked to open a meeting with prayer and became frozen with fear lost for words and confusion. I made a gesture to the organizer; I don't remember what, but he quickly started the prayer. It wasn't until this moment that I finally decided to check my (I'm ok) at the door and to seek out help. Even the council needs counseling at one time or another. A comforter needs comforting at seasons, and the minster needs a word meant especially for their wellbeing. During my *journey back* as I like to refer to my peace and healing, God gave me a word to write and create. Without a doubt; I understood that there was a book on the inside that needed to be written. During writing *Word therapy* was created. *Parental Loss and Grief Christian Counseling for the Grieving heart through Word Therapy* was birthed as a guide to ministering to the hurting through scripture as the ultimate reference material. The book came about out of a desire to share a basic yet detailed approach to healing the hurting through scripture.

INTRODUCTION

We all understand that each person is different; conversely everyone responds differently to crisis. Parental loss is the toughest of crisis, and there are no sure guidelines or markers that will determine how a parent will respond to the physical pain of losing a child of any age. Life experiences, gender, personality each can play a part in the way that we grieve. It is often difficult to council those who have experienced such a traumatic event. This book was written for the those who minister to and counsel the hurting. The material provides Christian faith-based methods to encourage a measure of wholeness. By covering the phases of grief, the reader will discover how to identify the various stages, and levels of grief to determine the most effective approach to the client or congregation **member. In an office setting or place of worship, the method of** *Word Therapy* **has been developed to individualize the care for the hurting. The material offers a step-by-step approach using** God's word, and scriptural references as the foundation. There is no timeline for grief, **again each person is different especially a husband and wife. Gaining knowledge on the right approach to a bereaved couple together, and as individuals is outlined using** God's word for healing as a powerful and proven tool. I sincerely hope that the book is a useful tool in ministry and counseling to bless the lives of others who you guide through the healing process.

CHAPTER 1

Find Strength in Adversity

So, do not fear, for I am with you; do not be dismayed, for I am your God. I will strengthen you and help you; I will uphold you with my righteous right hand."

— Isaiah 41:10 (NIV)

The Unexpected

Of all memories that may be, the first time that a parent holds their child is the happiest. This memorable event is met with profound optimism that this perfect gift from God is welcomed by the new parents. The mind of the parent adjusts to the opportunity to love and to nurture this amazing addition to the family.

Regardless of the event or cause, the whole world changes through a parent's lenses with the loss of a child. The loss of a child causes your very heartbeat to cease, as the intense hurt engulfs the entire body. No words can adequately describe the myriad of feelings that bombard the mind when the death of a child occurs. Experiencing an event of such intensity is so impactful that it is common to have your physical wellness negatively affected.

The Unimaginable

No parent expects to bury a child. The outright unfairness of such loss will definitely give rise to some anger. This anger is only natural. However, as nature and human interactions go, anger is indeed unnerving at times, even to your closest family. From the moment the loss of a child is confirmed, the mourning and recovery journey begins. Realistically, due to the profound love and attachment to your child, this journey never ends.

The loss of a child puts a grieving parent in a unique emotional state. In this scenario, grief is much different than the loss of any other relationship. The pain is out of this world. For example, there is the challenge of dealing with so many unanswered questions. In addition, every moment spent without the child brings about an inexplicable feeling of emptiness and the void of unbearable detachment. The loss of a blessing that is a child imminently sets in motion all manner of feelings and pain that can't really be described.

"I don't think of him every day, I think of him every hour." - Gregory Peck

The Undeniable Grace

The late actor Gregory Peck attempted to express the emptiness that ensues after the death of a son. Such a death leaves this overwhelming vacuum. The absence of a personality that formed an everyday part of our lives is, in itself, tough to bear. This I can relate to after suffering the loss of a child. The feelings that come with the circumstances during the grieving process or right after the loss of a child are immense. Guilt often manifests. It is the inherent nature of a parent to feel a duty to protect their child; and death, no matter the form, can bring about a feeling of failure. The parent thinks: *"I should have or could have done more to save my child."* In all this emotional upheaval, it is inevitable that all facets of your life will be affected. Such loss will have a parent embarking on a long, arduous, and mostly lonely journey. This search for peace of mind and acceptance will see a grieving parent, as well as couples, stand out from other individuals.

Regardless of the manner in which the death of a child came about, the loss will test a parent in ways they may never have imagined. Due to variation in personalities, each person will experience individual methods or channels of grieving; healing will vary from one person to another. With varying perceptions of painful feelings, it is necessary to vary the methodology employed in dealing with grief and loss.

In the event of loss, a great support system is not only good to have in place, but crucial for coping. This framework is set up as bereavement ministry, close family involvement, individual grief counseling or a professionally-led support group. These basic pillars of support for a parent in mourning serve very important purposes. They cover an array of key areas to set one on the path to healing.

CHAPTER 2

Bereavement and Comfort

"Rejoice with those who rejoice; mourn with those who mourn."

– Romans 12:15

Helping Hands Heal

This platform is available in church families. It reaches out and facilitates healing by intervening, providing immediate comfort and care for those experiencing any type of loss, especially bereavement. Death not only brings pain, among other emotions, but it also increases duties and responsibilities as well. For the grieving parent, this can very easily be overwhelming and confusing.

The loss of focus that comes during planning for how to cope during this time complicates any subsequent arrangements even further. The on-call or assigned Bereavement or Comfort Minister can be contacted at any time at any number of locations. This person must be ready to provide ministry support with a compassionate heart and sincere desire to minister to the hurting. Making house calls is one of the key functions of the ministry. Visits to the home(s) for the bereaved are planned, and the ministry oversees this initiative. With the unique needs that arise during the devastating circumstances of losing a child, some people will feel the need to share in order to shed some weight off their shoulders. Others will prefer to listen to any words that cultivate peace in their hearts. This initiative ensures that the ministry is availed to the individuals and couples that need it during their most trying time.

Bearing the Burden

"Bear one another's burdens, and so fulfil the law of Christ."

– Galatians 6:2

Being a Christian will not mean that we are free from the pain of loss. Jesus Himself witnessed and personally knew grief. *"When Jesus therefore saw her weeping, and the Jews also weeping which came with her, he groaned in the spirit, and was troubled, And said, Where have ye laid him? They said unto him, Lord, come and see. Jesus wept."*- John 11:33-36

Loss brings about the feeling of frailty or the lack of coordination to perform basic, everyday tasks. The Bereavement or Comfort Ministry is able to provide additional information and church contacts to take some of the burden off of the bereaved. These services greatly free up time for the grieving parent to attend to the difficult task ahead.

The Bereavement or Comfort Minister may also be available to provide follow-up counseling or refer the bereaved to the church's counseling center. Support at this stage of the healing process is critical. However, it may take weeks, months, or even years before a parent seeks out counseling.

Perfect Peace

We should remember that the comfort ministry within the church family is one of the first places a grieving parent will find unconditional assurance through Word Therapy. This is a setup that specifically aligns with our faith in God, and where His grace remains manifest through scripture. This ministry is effective to a great extent. Many occasions call for one to give it a proper chance in the midst of the myriad of emotions that are bombarding the grieving parent at the time. Trying times such as these can indeed bring us closer to God's healing grace, where His mercies endure forever. All peace and hope in the soul of a believer is rooted in the conviction that we have The Alpha and Omega looking out for us; and whenever we walk through the deep waters, we shall not be overwhelmed.

CHAPTER 3

Family Matters

"And the second is like, namely this, Thou shalt love thy neighbour as thyself. There is none other commandment greater than these."

– Mark 12:31

Family First

Family is undoubtedly the most compact unit in society. Bonds established by blood and other family ties give a unique connection. After the death of a child, family is usually the first and most important support framework. The existing bond between family members provides an environment that facilitates sharing and an essential safe space. It may be easier to talk with or listen to a trusted family member about grief and loss.

The death of a child can leave one feeling a need to isolate themselves and grieve in privacy. Despite this feeling, the healing process will most likely be accelerated by opening up and sharing feelings with someone. However, when one is bereaved and wants that space, convincing him or her to share may prove futile. It is at this point that a trusted family member proves key. An existing relationship of trust brings about a feeling of security, and subsequently the confidence to speak out and unburden the spirit.

Loving Kindness

Empathy and support from family can be genuine and profound. This sincere support is because family members personally share the grief of the bereaved individual or family, because the departed is a member of the family circle. Members in this group will usually be the first to respond, provide essential support, and form a crucial part of the healing process. When everyone else isn't obliged to stay after the funeral, family can remain the ever-present support system. Close relations will always step in, especially where external intervention is not expected, or fails to live up to expectations, in this particularly trying time.

Grief Support Groups

The grief and mourning process is frequently misunderstood. It is common to feel left out after the loss of a child. A general perception that others cannot relate to the pain or emotion that comes with the loss is likely to set in. A challenge of this nature can vex, with the need to facilitate a safe environment arising. Support groups offer a unique opportunity to meet others who can relate to a similar loss and understand what a grieving person is going through.

Here are the main benefits of a grief support group:

- Physical and emotional support is available in a safe environment.
- There is comfort in being in a group with others who are dealing with a similar loss.

- A support group gives the grieving parent(s) an opportunity to share and listen to others who have experienced the loss of a child as well.
- One learns crucial coping skills to help manage the challenges that come with the death of a child.
- A grieving parent will easily feel understood in such a setup.
- It is easy to observe how others have reacted to their loss and practiced their coping mechanisms.
- Insight comes about regarding how to honor and preserve the memory of a child.
- The safe environment makes it easier for one to truly grieve openly when comfortable in the setting.

It is vital to make use of support systems available in this difficult time, with healing usually being a process that requires incredible patience and one that guarantees to test you to the limit.

CHAPTER 4

Christian Grief and Christian Word Therapy

*"He heals the brokenhearted
And binds up their wounds [healing their pain and comforting their sorrow]."*

– Psalms 147:3 (AMP)

A Common Place

By common bonds and virtue of being human, everyone will undoubtedly mourn the loss of a loved one. After such loss, various avenues are employed to seek peace and healing. Personal faith will play a crucial part on our perception of loss and will ultimately dictate how the mourning, grief and healing process will be managed. Faith in God helps us to grieve and seek healing with God's promise of hope. Absence of this spiritual connection to God will many times aggravate the sorrow and hopelessness. Peace and assurance come through the promises in the Word of God.

"Be strong and take heart, all you who hope in the Lord."

– Psalm 31:24 (NIV)

In our nature as spiritual beings, our understanding of God's Word is essential on the road to healing. Continuous assurance and a never-ending array of guidelines for comfort and peace is made available through His Word. Spiritual and mental healing are the desired goals, with scripture giving word on how to handle loss of a child.

Christian Word Therapy therefore, is essential for true healing and restoration to take place. Christian counseling with scripture as the basis of guidance will encourage change, empathy, and genuine peace.

Strength in Numbers

"Where there is no guidance, a people falls, but in an abundance of counselors there is safety."

— Proverbs 11:14 (KJV)

The Word advocates for guidance as a key ingredient to healing. After loss, the opportunity to counsel and care should be promptly seized. However, it is true that the grieving parent will seek out counseling when they are ready, which means this may not occur during the mourning process or correspond with the timing of those in their circle.

This undertaking of pursuing counseling should be initiated on purpose, as pain and grief affects believers and non-believers the same way. The Word of God explicitly outlines the importance of counselors, without whom failure is inevitable. Counseling helps assure one who is grieving, especially with the overwhelming grief that follows the passing of a son or daughter.

CHAPTER 5

Childlike Faith

"For this child I prayed, and the Lord has granted me my petition that I made to Him. Therefore I have lent him to the Lord. As long as he lives, he is lent to the Lord…"

– 1 Samuel 1:27-28

"…But as for me and my household, we will serve the Lord."

– Joshua 24:15

Faith for Life

Losing a child of any age can be unbearable. A conflict will be clearly evident in the spirit as all manner of emotions and feelings take center stage.

In this tumultuous mental state, the true value represented by the brief moments you had the opportunity to share thoughts and feelings with your child will be felt. Greater will be the feeling of emptiness when a child passes on.

Children are a blessing; every Christian parent will have prayed for the young soul even before birth, as was the case with Samuel's birth when his mother Hannah dedicated him:

The children born to a believer are a blessing, one that is cause for joy and dedication. The birth of your child is also the birth of a purpose-driven being; it is the introduction of a soul born into intended service to God. Untimely death, therefore, is and will continue to be viewed as an unfulfilled destiny, and as an incomplete life. In these two scriptures, the role of birth and family service to God is laid out. This role is cut short when a child passes on, and Word Therapy and counseling oversee true and complete healing and restoration. Make no mistake, the loss of a child will be felt, even after substantial healing has taken place, since the death of a special one doesn't imply erasure from memory.

Faith for Mourning

WebMD describes grief as: 'A natural response to death or loss. The grieving process is an opportunity to appropriately mourn a loss and then heal.' Loss and grief are inevitable in life. The death of a loved one is devastating, having deep and long-lasting effects on the bereaved. It is in this loss that, yet again, scripture offers solid reassurance:

"Fear not, for I am with you; be not dismayed, for I am your God; I will strengthen you, I will help you, I will uphold you with my righteous hand."

– Isaiah 41:10 (NIV)

Grief has five phases, and a parent, guardian or couple mourning the loss of a child are likely to undergo each stage, though not always.

The five stages of grief are:

I. Denial and isolation

II. Anger

III. Bargaining

IV. Depression

V. Acceptance

The life-shattering experience of having to bury a child will need a structured path to recovery. Any and all processes need intensive support and proper, scheduled follow-ups. Of key importance is the adherence to Biblical guidelines for true edification and healing. The effect of death on the bereaved is unnatural, and the subsequent healing process will be rooted on healing the wounded soul through Christian Word Therapy.

CHAPTER 6

Words Matter

"Gracious words are a honeycomb, sweet to the soul and healing to the bones."

– Proverbs 16:24 (NIV)

The Gravity of Your Words

The loss of a child sparks a lot of feelings and emotional turmoil. A parent will lose interest in a lot of things that make up his or her daily routine. The siblings and close family will inevitably suffer as well. It is at this time that everyone arrives to offer words of comfort and show empathy to the bereaved. It is not unusual to have increased activity in the home as friends, family, workmates, and members of the church, among others, throng the home in a show of support. On arrival, with the general pleasantries done, the floor is open for condolences. Talking to someone who has been shattered by the death of a child calls for not only tact, but wisdom. The choice of words matters a lot. What you say to someone dealing with great loss can make the situation much better or bring more anger and pain. Anytime you are on such a ministry counseling visit, it helps to think about what needs to be said, so that your moments with the grieving parent(s) bring some healing. The Bible calls for a wise choice of words in addressing different situations. It is, therefore, critical that you get some scriptural backing as you visit a fellow believer who is trying to come to terms with the loss of their child. Insight from the book of Proverbs likens gracious or kind words to a honeycomb that is sweet to the soul. This first part of the verse highlights the sweetness of the words. Not only do they excite the soul, but they have a general soothing impact. The same verse says that they are healing to the bones. This reference is testimony to the ability of words to breathe new life into a person or situation. In the Valley of Dry Bones, Ezekiel was told to prophesy to the bones in the desolate valley (Ezekiel: Chapter 37). Bones are a metaphor for great loss and situations that are beyond comprehension. Deep down, that feeling is only part of what the bereaved feel. Your kind words will bring some life to the parent's spirit. It is critical to know that words can have a positive or negative impact, depending on the choice and application. *Life and death are in the power of the tongue, and they that love it shall eat the fruit thereof." – Proverbs 18:21 (KJV)*

The Weight of Your Words

The Bible offers constant encouragement to consistently say what is constructive to the audience, which is a choice of words that bring about grace and calmness to the listener. The words also need to be suitable for the occasion. This means that good words don't necessarily suit every situation.

"Do not let any unwholesome talk come from your mouths, but only what is helpful for building others up according to their needs, that it may benefit those who listen." – Ephesians 4:29 (NIV) Being considerate isn't the only reason to offer kind words to those who need it, but such timely

support is, in itself, obedience of a Biblical directive.

It is critical, however, to note that as much as we may intend to heal and comfort with the Word, it is imperative that one doesn't turn a visit to the grieving into a sermon. The company and the right combination of intense listening and kind words are what prove vital for the visit to be truly effective.

CHAPTER 7

Choice of Words Wisely

"Death and life are in the power of the tongue: ..."
Proverbs 18:21

Unhelpful Words for a Grieving Parent

There are words that sound good and kind but are ultimately unsuitable for use during a visit to a grieving parent or couple. It is important to note that these words may even have a Christian connotation. But, suitability is everything; and therefore, wisdom and tact are of key significance.

Here is a selection of words or phrases that should be avoided:

- **"He or she is in a better place now."**

A child is born to grow up and benefit from the experience and wisdom of the parent(s). Untimely, death of a child of any age distorts the process. A parent is no longer able to nurture the young soul and grow their spirit and intellect, instilling good virtue. In this perspective, a child's place is in the constant company and guidance of the mother, father or both. It may offer you solace if heaven is part of your faith, but it is simply unsuitable for the situation.

As Christians, we understand the Bible promise that our grief will be temporary, while our joy will be forever; we have the hope of being reunited with our child. I personally understand that we would selfishly prefer our child be here with us, rather than with the Father. For this reason, you must be mindful to avoid offering such a statement to a grieving parent. More than knowledge, you must realize that wisdom and tact play a critical role in carefully picking what we say to the bereaved.

- **"I know (exactly) how you feel."**

Uhhmm... no you don't. You honestly have no idea of what someone is dealing with or feeling, as they try to come to terms with the loss of their child. Grieving parents will be, at that point, dealing with the greatest challenge of their lives, with so much emotional and spiritual turmoil. It is unwise to presume, and even worse to say, that you understand exactly what they feel. Your presence and support at this trying time is what is required. Even if you have lost a child yourself, as I have—and there may be parallels—each person grieves differently. Never put yourself into the equation. However, you may be challenged with the question: "Have you lost a child?" If so, go ahead and answer honestly and then refocus to the task of guiding the parent(s) through their grief to healing through the Word.

- **"I experienced something similar."**

Always understand that the parent(s) of the recently departed child are grieving. Focus of helping them manage the situation is essential. To re-emphasize, regardless of whether you have experienced the loss of a child yourself, this is not the time to draw similarities between the two events. It only trivializes feelings of the parent in grief. It is their time to mourn their loved one, and it is crucial that you have a proper choice of words that focus on helping them stay calm and start healing.

- **"This or that stage of grieving will last x months."**

Always avoid highlighting stages of grief to those in mourning. There is no set timeline to mourn the loss of a loved one, especially when death strikes at a young age. One should take all the time they feel necessary in coming to terms with such significant loss. It's crucial to avoid any utterance that implies prescribed timelines for someone's healing process. Part of the assurance healing will take place is guaranteeing someone that they have the freedom to take as much time as necessary to learn to live with the recent turn of events.

- **"It's not that bad."**

Never try and downplay the severity of the situation, hoping that the bereaved will somehow get strength from it. Death is bad. Regardless of the age of the child or the circumstances, the situation is not to be casually dismissed in hopes of helping a grieving parent move on. A loss of this magnitude will bring about all manner of challenges and pain to the parents and family of the deceased. Such statements that try to belittle the tragic loss of a young life should be avoided at all times.

- **"She/he was so good that God had to take him or her."**

Parents savor every minute spent with their children. The chief aspect of togetherness is continued company and unlimited interaction.

Despite the seemingly Christian connotation of this statement, it is likely to do more harm than good. Every parent deserves time with their child, and any statement that seems to downplay or minimize that need for companionship is guaranteed to evoke some mixed feelings.

CHAPTER 8

Healing Words

"He sent his word, and healed them, and delivered them from their destructions."

Psalms 107:20

Helpful Words for a Grieving Parent

After this unfortunate tragedy, it is important to be genuine with your sentiments and words of comfort. Whatever you say should be heartfelt and from a real place in your soul. This emotional and sincere backing gives your words power. Anything uttered that lacks conviction will sound forced and pretentious, and will have minimal or no effect—perhaps even be unwelcomed. When comforting someone, the tone and emotion of your words determine the level of impact your consolation effort will have. Paul's directive on outreach and sharing the Word refers to a foundation of true love.

"The goal of this command is love, which comes from a pure heart and a good conscience and sincere faith."

– 1 Timothy 1:5 (NIV)

In consoling a parent after such loss, it is important to avoid trying to personally fix their emotional status, but rather offer genuine support. Healing is essentially a personal journey; the people around those in mourning only facilitate the process by timely and strategic intervention. A sincere tone will be welcome, because it helps the grieving party to relax emotionally and this will encourage them to open up and talk, which is a vital part of the healing process.

Here is a selection of calculated words to use:

- **"I can't begin to imagine how tough this is for you."**

It is established that you don't have any idea just how weighed down and hurt someone is by the tragic loss of their child. A sincere statement that you will not pretend to have their troubles figured out is a great approach to starting the consolation process. The last thing a hurting person needs is pretense and inaccurate sentiments. This statement can also be interpreted to imply your understanding that the magnitude of the situation is too great to fully comprehend, which is not only honest but accurate as well.

- **"I am so sorry for your loss."**

This is the ultimate sincere condolence. It expresses sympathy and the genuine need to stand with the grieving parent. It may seem too common and cliché, but when said from a real place, it has such a great impact in comforting someone. It shows understanding that one has lost an irreplaceable part of themselves. The wording that involves 'I am so sorry' is perfect to express the heartfelt sympathy being passed on to those in mourning.

- **At the right moment, you may reach out.**

There is no time table that determines when a grieving parent will seek counseling. This can occur at any time during the 5 stages of grief, even during the final stage of acceptance. It is imperative to plan for how to approach all stages through Word Therapy. Some parents may seek counseling because they need a sounding board outside of their circle. Others may be looking for a biblical approach to dealing with their loss, while others may seek Christian Counseling because of a family intervention.

Blessed are those who mourn, for they shall be comforted: Matthew 5:4.

- **Offer your silence (listen).**

When comforting a parent after such a tragedy, you should avoid the temptation to try and fill in the blanks with speech. Always remember that peace and tranquility often come by being heard—through your listening. The silence allows the parent time to express their feelings and memories. The parent, since the lost, has only heard the constant chatter of family, friends and co-worker condolences. This is their time; respect it. Silence is the only constant in the healing process, and its significance cannot be overemphasized.

- **Give scriptural encouragement.**

It goes without saying that someone who has lost of child is a challenging client without God's Word. Your purpose is to share kind words with the assurance of unconditional support. This human connection gives a foundation for your input in someone's healing process. They have to emotionally let you in before they can properly absorb any words that are said, after the initial interaction. The amount of scriptures used should also be wisely monitored. Too many will have your visit feeling like a sermon, and this contradicts the purpose of your company.

"He will wipe every tear from their eyes. There will be no more death, or mourning, or crying, or pain, for the old order of things has passed away."

– Revelations 21:4 (NIV)

"Even though I walk through the darkest valley, I will fear no evil, for you are with me; your rod and your staff, they comfort me."

– Psalms 23:4 (NIV)

The Holy Spirit is the comforter of those in Christ. The scripture shared will augment your words of comfort for the grieving; and, scripture effectively complements your condolences, as it revives the spirit of the one hurting. Strength comes from the connection to scriptural promises, finding root on a divine platform that quells the pain and confusion.

"My flesh and my heart may fail, but God is the strength of my heart and my portion forever."

– Psalm 73:6 (NIV)

"You Lord, keep my lamp burning; my God turns my darkness into light."

– Psalm 18:28 (NIV)

- **"Make yourself available."**

During a period that bears so much anger, confusion, and a myriad of tumultuous emotions, a grieving parent may feel left out and trapped. Keeping all this pain and confusion inside can be devastating. Venting and finding an outlet for all this is vital. It cleanses the soul, where without judgment, audience is granted. A huge burden is shed by asking questions out loud, airing your aches, or simply letting the tears flow. The assurance that you are willing to give your time and company is very comforting and reduces the feeling of isolation when another person is dealing with grief.

To supplement our words in the process of consoling someone, the overall conduct during the visit should also reflect the solidarity and empathy we speak of. On a visit, always strive to paint a picture of approachability and one of someone genuinely willing to listen.

It is crucial that we also learn to listen to the person we are trying to counsel. The risk of making an exchange in such situations one-sided is constant. It goes a long way when we properly identify the perfect moment to stop talking and listen. Allowing the bereaved party to speak is a prime avenue for healing and finding peace, and it goes a long way to remember that it is during one of your visits that a lot of this speaking is destined to take place.

The impact of your words will not be simply dependent on the nature of what you say or when you say it, but impact also comes from what you do to cement your intentions to truly empathize with the grieving parent(s). Find the perfect balance between words and actions, and your gestures of comfort and encouragement will be that much more effective. Maintaining this delicate balance ensures that what we project outward, when comforting the bereaved, manifests its desired effect, infinitely bettering the situation; we become the agents of comfort and healing.

CHAPTER 9

The Five Phases of Grief

Overcoming grief and attaining true healing is a process. Pain and hurt will evolve and change, and as time passes by, a strategic approach is necessary so that a grieving parent can find peace and come to terms with the loss. The essence of this process is to take reasonable time at each phase, with application of the correct approaches at each level. In many scenarios, stagnation for a prolonged period at a select stage will mean that the healing process is hampered. This delay in progression may be hindered as a result of an improper approach to the situation, or due to the influence of other external factors adding to the emotional challenges the bereaved one is already dealing with. For true healing to take place, the emotional support system has to be sound. This involves timely and correct intervention. The components of this support system will usually involve friends, family, colleagues, grief support groups, and the bereavement or comfort ministry. Continued support after the burial of the child has been characteristically absent, and this has made dealing with loss more challenging. The presence and level of support that was availed right after death and was confirmed up to the date of burial suddenly withers, leaving the mourning parent abandoned and still hurting, trying to figure out the next best move. As we offer our support, we must ensure that we employ speech and thought that has biblical backing.

Word Therapy: A Necessity

Use of scripture in ministering to those in pain ensures that we not only help them feel better, but as Christian Counselors, we minister to their spirit as well, uplifting and rejuvenating them.

The support and compassion that we extend is reciprocation of God's infinite grace for us. The Word instructs us to comfort those facing trying times, just as God's never-ending love and compassion has been made available to us.

"Praise be to the God and Father of our Lord Jesus Christ, the Father of compassion and the God of all Comfort, who comforts us in all our troubles, so that we can comfort those in any trouble with the comfort we ourselves receive from God."

– 2nd Corinthians 1:3-4 (NIV)

We must therefore, at all times, be willing to comfort those in need of healing and peace as a divine responsibility.

The Kübler-Ross Model

Elisabeth Kübler-Ross articulated the stages of grief, applicable to death in her book *On Death and Dying, published in 1969.* She articulates what people experience after it dawns on them that someone they love is dying. Carefully mapped, it covers the initial reaction of shock or denial of the inevitable, all the way to the moment of acceptance. It is critical that we realize that this isn't a one-size-fits-all platform, as different individuals will tend to handle grief in varied ways. This variation in personality means that the linear progression as outlined will not always be followed. It is a real possibility that someone dealing with grief will also likely fail to feel in a linear fashion what is outlined in the model.

Dr. Kübler-Ross later clarified that the theory isn't meant to be applied in the perceived linear manner for everyone, citing that just as individuals are unique, their experiences at select phases will be different. The order and personal experiences in the designated stages will therefore vary. The influence of past challenges will also be felt in the way someone deals with the loss of a son or daughter; it may aggravate pain or ensure a more level-headed approach. In whichever situation a grieving person finds himself/herself, pain will be constant.

Stage 1: Denial

It is in us to subconsciously reject the idea of something bad happening to us. This is especially true in a situation of the magnitude of losing a child. We picture a perfect life in an imperfect world where, hopefully, everything will work out just fine. The expectation is that we'll live, and our children will as well. We go as far as planning ahead, looking forward to birthday parties, recitals, soccer games, and even graduations, and beyond. When a child passes, all of these expectations are thrown in disarray. Everything we anticipated to be fulfilled is snuffed out in one tragic moment. The heart is defiant, and the mind will confront all manner of questions about the unwelcome passing of a young soul.

At this stage, the grieving party will tend to remain isolated, as they strive to find meaning in what just happened. Discussions about the current events will be generally unwelcome at this point. Wisdom dictates that you refrain from digging up all the painful details about what, when and how everything happened. The best approach in comforting someone at this stage is simply giving your company, heartfelt condolences, and any practical and financial assistance you see necessary. In its nature, this is a brief stage. Denial doesn't last too long for the simple reason that reality tends to set in fast. After a while, one begins to see evidence of the current situation all around. In the latter stages of this phase, the initial process of reaching out and trying to cope begins. The bereaved will call to inform friends, family and the church about the unfortunate turn of events.

However, denial will last long in select cases, as a parent tries to find peace and comfort in the notion that the child's presence is still a reality. Evidently, such an approach will not always cause more pain. The defiance to believe in the tragic loss of a young life may bring about some peace.

Stage 2: Anger

Death will have a parent feeling a great sense of injustice. *Why me? What did I do to deserve all this? What did my child do to deserve death at such a young age?* A deep-set sense of unfairness will set in, and anger will promptly follow. This resentment is rooted in all the unfulfilled dreams, soccer games that never were, the wedding that turned out to be a fantasy, the unexpected demise. It's crucial to realize that the person is in indescribable pain, trying to get all these weird emotions sorted. Therefore, it would be unfair to think that someone is genuinely snapping at you. It takes patience, understanding, and lots of tolerance, to withstand the anger of someone who has suffered loss. Any impatience can prompt a third party to walk away, finding the situation abhorrent, despite the good intentions that prompted the initial contact.

This phase will be relatively brief as well. However, as we have an infinite array of personalities, some people will hold onto the anger that results from loss. Some people will even die angry. In itself, anger can be devastating; and it is advisable to find a way to channel that anger and keep it in check. Anger may push one to harm themselves or others; it is destructive. Anger is responsible for loss of peace and will generally not allow you to fondly remember someone, or even be grateful for the incredible blessing their brief presence was. With every unforeseen loss, anger is a consistent component of the grieving process. It is, however, destructive when not dealt with within a reasonable time, with all chances of true healing jeopardized.

Stage 3: Bargaining

Bargaining will be an alternative approach, employed when anger doesn't bear the desired effect. Take the example of a child trying to get something from the mother. When the mother responds with a plain no, the characteristic tantrum and throwing toys will follow. However, with time, the keen child will realize that the situation calls for a different approach. They will try to bargain:

"If you get me xyz, I will keep my room clean."

"If you take me out for ice-cream, I will do all my chores on time."

The goal of bargaining is to get something in return from another, from giving something that you feel is within your ability to provide or avail. One will repeatedly hope that the loss is nothing but a bad dream, promising never to sleep again if they wake up from it.

For Christians, bargaining will be done with God. The bereaved party will promise to live a good life, to offer help to the needy, keep their faith in the right place, if God will take their pain away. Bargaining is, in itself, a normal reaction to pain and grief. When one is going to bargain, in order to change a reality, it is the evidence of going through a devastating phase. It is inadvertently admitting that the situation is beyond human ability to correct, needing divine intervention. On a practical basis, it doesn't bear any tangible fruit many times, but remains a very evident phase on the road to recovery.

Stage 4: Depression

Depression sets in when one starts to realize the extent of the pain and loss. When you have lost someone, it may take a while to realize the severe nature of the situation, as you try to deny and bargain your way out of your predicament. After all the bargaining hasn't worked, you start to see a clearer picture, and the extent of the loss becomes more evident by the day. It is at this point that the pain of tragedy overwhelms you and depression sets in. Depression is characterized by a lack of interest in daily activities that formed the routine before loss: easy aggravation, a need to isolate oneself, and a general lack of the feeling of self-worth.

In this phase, Dr. Kübler-Ross highlighted two types of depression:

- Reactive depression – this occurs as one reacts to the current situation or past losses. It comes about as an effect of the death of the child, for instance. It is more of a reflex to bad circumstances. The state of your surroundings will slide one into a depressive state as their mind tries to bear all the pain. The present is brought into sharp perspective, and everything that is perceived to be out of place hurts the spirit. Reactive depression is likely to bring about a lot of anger, denial, and general disarray to one's peace of mind. Everything that surrounds the loss, including the probable or established cause of the loss, will be subjected to blame and resentment.

- Preparatory depression – this type of depression is brought about by the concern of what the future holds, as a result of death and loss. It is primarily rooted in fear. The anticipation of challenges and a painful present evokes fear of what's to come. This depression is born of anxiety for the future, with all the uncertainties laid out, appearing overwhelming and with seemingly no way to escape the painful times to come. Being human, the future is a constant item in our inner deliberations, and unexpected loss dims the promise of better times, sullying the present as well.

"Do not be anxious about anything, but in every situation, with prayer and petition, with thanksgiving, present your requests to God. And the peace of God, which transcends all understanding, will guard your hearts and your minds in Christ Jesus."

— Philippians 4:6-7 (NIV)

"But I trust in your unfailing love, my heart rejoices in your salvation."

— Psalm 13:5

Fear and anxiety are the core causes of preparatory depression. It is difficult not to worry considering the circumstances, but the Word comforts us and encourages us to find solace in divine peace. It is God's promise to love, heal, and beautify us. In our most trying times, it is a divine assurance that in The Almighty, we will find our redemption and salvation through healing of the soul and spirit.

Stage 5: Acceptance

When all is said and done, one will go through a lot of emotional pain and turmoil. This feeling of hurt is bound to last for a while. However, in one defining moment, peaceful resolution begins to set in. This is the moment that allows one to admit that any pain or loss that happened has come to pass, and faith in healing and peace is ignited. All the feelings of grief have been let out by this time, and the bereaved will have made active progress in making amends. On acceptance, a grieving parent will exhibit signs of recovery from grief, find a more level platform emotionally, and start to take active steps in picking up the pieces.

Acceptance signals the entry of genuine peace. It is characterized by healing of the spirit, and true calm will soothe the soul. The presence of continued anger, resentment or guilt after the loss of a loved one greatly delays the entry of acceptance and peace. Failure to accept will also affect the immediate family, with talk of the deceased proving to be a touchy, disruptive and divisive topic in general. Denial may continue for longer periods and may subsequently see the bereaved clinging onto items that represent the physical presence of the departed. This will include keeping their rooms untouched and even locked for decades. The idea of keeping everything intact masks reality, offering an alternative reality that the child is still around.

The 5-stage model by Dr. Kübler-Ross is comprehensive in many situations, when you are dealing with the loss of a loved one or those diagnosed with terminal illnesses. One should remember that as we are all different, the reaction to tragic loss of life will vary. Some individuals will have great mental strength do deal with such trying times, prompting those around them to wonder if they are aware of the severity of the situation. The simple truth is that grief is constant, and it's that much more overwhelming after the loss of a child. What remains evident is that healing is a process. If we are part of the support system looking to bring peace and healing, patience and wisdom are key as we seek to help bear the burden of loss. All elements in the healing process are critical, with the need to make the most out of each for a more complete recovery.

Applying God's Word to a grieving heart is power because there is *Power in the Word of God.* While some may differ, the loss of a child is unique in the sense that the loss goes against everything we expect in life. Christian Word Therapy is designed to address the pain, applying the scriptures to the fact that the parent will experience the five stages of grief. Grief and its effects differ from one person to the other, and there is no set timeline for grief. While healing is possible, the parent will forever feel the void of their child. The process to recovery is often long and trying; and, more than anything that can be availed by the usual support systems, we need

God's intervention for the heart and soul to be truly whole.

CHAPTER 10

Word Therapy Tool Kit

PHASE 1: THOUGHTS
- *Remember*
- *Repentance*
- *Rediscover*
- *Realign*

Remember

Memory is what a person reverts to upon discovering the death of a loved one. The memory bank is so full that memories are often distorted at the beginning of the grief process. Memories of the past are intertwined with the cause of the passing. When this happens, our ultimate response might be complete denial. It is difficult to believe that the person is no longer alive. We remember the sound of their voice, their personality, our conversations with them, perhaps an initial meeting, various moments in time, and exchanges we had with that individual. We *find it difficult* to accept the finality of their life. We *struggle* to embrace the new normal.

THE APPROACH

Here is where we will introduce some mental strategies to help those who are grieving. They will need to wrap their minds around the idea of a new reality. The approach will include case studies on the science of the three target areas we plan to minister to the grieving individual and/or family:

1. Denial

2. Refusal

3. Struggle

Repentance

Shortly after the reality sets in that our loved one has passed away, we may be feel a sense of guilt. We may be guilty because we should have been there; guilty, because we should have known; guilty, because we could have stopped it; guilty, because we didn't get the chance to say good-bye. No matter how our loved one transitioned, there is a sense of ownership that leads us to repentance. We *wish* we could go back and change the hands of time. We *desire* to say something, do something, or fix something that could have prevented the death. We may feel *convicted,* because we may think it should have been us instead.

THE APPROACH

Here is where we bring the grieving to a place of wholeness. Repentance is a natural response, but there is a supernatural result that comes from this time of reflection. Our goal is to bring understanding and peace, as well as to help release the guilt and shame that grows in the heart, when mourning or repentance is unbridled.

1. Wish
2. Desire
3. Conviction

I love this: repentance is a hard word for some to embrace. It is difficult for some to make the connection between the grief-related feelings, emotions and thoughts and repentance (turning away).

Rediscover

Repentance can bring us to our knees and rediscovery can bring us to our feet. It is said that time heals all wounds. While it is said, it is not written. The written Word says earth has no sorrow that heaven cannot heal. Heaven is not limited to time. Time was made for man; man was not made for time. One cannot put a timeframe on how long to mourn or grieve. As believers in Christ, we do not grieve like the world, because we have a hope: a hope of glory. The time of rediscovery is not based on seconds, minutes, hours, days, weeks, months, or years. Our time of rediscovery is a revelation that brings a resolution.

THE APPROACH

Here is where we point the grieving away from the brain and into the mind. The brain has no understanding of spiritual things. Our mind has no understanding of natural things. If we are going to grow forward, we need a revelation. The goal is to help the grieving find the treasure in the wilderness experience.

1. Wilderness
2. Valley
3. Promise Land

Realign

Death can leave an immeasurable hole in our lives. A part of us dies when our loved one dies, and that can compound the measure of grief. They took our words with them. They took our experiences with them. They took our laughter with them. They took the sound of our voice with them. They took our memories with them. In the aftermath of death, we fight to find our experiences, laughter, voice, and memories. For some of us, our loved one took our appetite for food, desire for life, and passion for purpose. As we close the loop on the first phase of the Word response approach to grief, we will help the grieving gather up and realign the fragments in their lives, so there will be nothing lost.

THE APPROACH

Here is where we go for the strong close. This is the most important step of Phase 1, the ability to convert a broken heart. There is nothing lost in the kingdom of God. There is nothing broken in God – but His body, which was broken for us. Our approach is to help the grieving take and eat of the brokenness of God – broken for us. Eating out of every Word that proceeds from the mouth of God ensures we get the nutrients and healing agents that take life and color when we digest them.

1. See the Word
2. Hear the Word
3. Understand the Word of God

PHASE 2: SPEECH

- *Restore*
- *Recover*
- *Redeem*
- *Rebuild*

RESTORATION: *Speak the Word*

The first thing that the death of a love one does is take the breath away from those he or she leaves behind. A breath-taking experience, the gravity of death can leave one perplexed and saddened. Therapy is often frowned upon, because it is viewed by some to be a sign of weakness. In reality, therapy is for strength-building, not for fault-finding. The goal of therapy is to provide a safe environment where one can be open enough to express their emotions organically with one who has perception and experience in dealing with emotional trauma. The counselor can help us triage the catastrophic incidents we face, death being one of them.

Having a loss for words is an understatement when we face the passing of a loved one. The first step in the healing process is to find a way to become a good steward over our words. While we want to be as authentic as possible in sharing our most intimate feelings, we are cognizant of the fact that God's Word still has final authority in our lives. As Word therapists, we offer a well-balanced approach to the grieving process that is both scriptural and natural. In our humanness, we mourn with those who mourn and stand in the gap for those who are weary from grief. A true revelation on prayer is what makes all the difference in the world during the implementation of Word therapy.

Prayer is an open dialogue between us and God. It is the positive affirmation of the finished work of Christ with a declarative voice of triumph. By this we know that we are not praying for an answer; our prayer is the answer. It is our answered prayer that we have a blood-bought right to be healed. The life of Jesus took on the cares of this world. The death of Jesus took the sting from death, hell and the grave. The resurrection of Jesus made us able ministers – receivers of His delegated authority to declare the scriptures and heal nations. If we are going to help those struggling with removing the sting of death, we must introduce them to a whole new vocabulary.

RECOVER: *The Parts of Speech*

The part of speech that is most effective in Word therapy is not what we say, as much as how we say it. How we say it is not about the rhythm or pronouncement of the words we speak, but having full faith and confidence in God every time we open our mouths to speak. Did you know that as ministers of this dispensation of God's grace, we are distribution channels for heaven's medicine for the soul? Yes, there is a balm in Gilead and it's resting, ruling, and abiding on the inside of you. Healing is on the tip of your tongue. God's Word is healing. It discerns the heart of a man and separates bone marrow from joints. While it is scientifically impossible for bone marrow to be separated from a joint, with God all things are possible. The words that you release are spirit, and they are life. You have the spirit of God living on the inside of you, and the healing that takes place in the earth starts with the Word of God that we speak.

We don't have to come up with anything. God has already said everything, and God's Word is true. We simply say what He said in Jeremiah 1:12, "You have seen well, because I am watching to fulfill my word." There will be no performance in the lives of those who are hurting, if we don't speak His Word. Speaking the Word doesn't mean we quote scripture. People don't care how much we know – they want to know how much we care. We know a lot of scripture but does the scripture know us? As ministers and comforters, we know that the Word of God must have a safe place in us to abide. We will not neglect or misrepresent the Word, but use it for its intended purpose. God's Word is infallible. We have been entrusted to refrain from watering it down, compromising it, or sending it out for any reason other than to accomplish the purpose of God's Word. The enemy also knows scripture, and will use it while cloaked in deception. The true Word of God provides a level of discernment and the promise of experiencing the abundant life, which means operating in the God kind of faith and obtaining healing.

REDEEM: *Word Currency*

Speaking the Word by faith is not a flesh and blood matter; it's a spiritually mature act of a believer. God has settled every matter and your heart is mending as we speak. There is no rest for the weary; so, we call your heart healed, your needs met, your tears counted, your voice triumphant, your love renewed, your problems solved, your ashes beauty, your heaviness joyful, and your poverty prosperous. The Word of our power causes supernatural change to come on the inside of those we serve. We acknowledge the hurt, frustration, anxiety, disappointment and depression that the earth causes with its sorrow, but only as a point of reference for the manifested healing that is taking place in their lives. When we speak the Word to the sick, we call for their body to recondition itself to expand its capacity to receive the supernatural. When we speak to the heavy-hearted, we acknowledge their suffering only as a means of recognizing a triumphant end; and, by the Word of our power, we call the spirit of God to run in and run over where we run out.

We announce openly that we are powerless, but that God has all power. We say that the hurt the family is experiencing today shall be a memory without a sting, when the manifested healing power of our God shows up and shows out, in and through their lives. We proclaim the sadness we know today to be an enemy we shall see no more. We call depression an enemy of God's grace and mercy, which we declare will follow us all the days of our lives, comforting us in times of distress and filling us up in days of unrest. When we speak with this authority, it shows the hearer that we are sympathetic to their plight, but we love them too much to leave them there.

REBUILD: *The End from the Beginning*

As ministers, we must always remember that we don't come to be a part. We come as we have been called. "And he gave some, apostles; and some, prophets; and some, evangelists; and some, pastors and teachers." *Ephesians 4:11 (NKJV)*

Anytime we are called to the bleeding side of the lost and broken-hearted, it is not to be a temporary Band-Aid, but we are called to restore life and affirm the joy of living. If the Word of

God is spirit and life, then we know that what we say is the currency that will bring healing to every broken place. We are not the healers; we are on a diplomatic assignment from heaven, deployed to the earth as a distribution channel of God's abundant wealth, of which healing is but a portion. His Kingdom comes on earth, as it is in heaven, to bind up and loose at our command. We have the delegated authority to represent Him, and to apply the authority to minister to the hurting.

When we speak the Word of God, we create an atmosphere of change. We are change agents in the earth and ambassadors of Christ. While ministering to a family who has just experienced loss can seem like a difficult task, God's work is not a burden; it is a pleasure. God never allows anything to grow without first creating the atmosphere conducive for its life and reproduction. When He created the garden in Eden, there was no man to dress the field, so God created Adam to cultivate it and guard the garden. God wants to manifest healing in the lives of His people, but He uses our voice to set the atmosphere. This makes healing possible, to not only live, but to reproduce after its own kind. God doesn't just want to heal the broken family; He wants to make us whole.

Once we have created an atmosphere for change, transformation is inevitable. Faith is an energy that is not lost or destroyed. It is supernaturally transferred from one heart to another. While the reality may say we are in mourning, scripture confirms that God allowed mourning for a time; but, it always has an expiration date. "For his anger endures but a moment; in his favor is life: weeping may endure for a night, but joy comes in the morning" *Psalm 30:5 (AKJV)*. As believers, we do not grieve like the world because we have a hope in Christ. Our goal is to transfer that hope into the lives of those whose lives we are assigned. And, the seeds we sewed in their hearts when they were open and vulnerable – while they didn't appear to be receptive – established spiritual changes, were rooted, and are now coming to harvest. This is why God is never concerned with what people say or think about His Word. He told Jeremiah to speak the Word to the people, and to never look at their faces nor listen to their words. His Word is seed. It is not like the world – offering quick reaction and instant gratification. It may not appear that the family hears one word you are saying, but know that the death of their loved one created an openness for God's Word to be sown, when it may not have otherwise been received. God's system of seed time and harvest is a process. The ground is cultivated, and seeds are sown; and in due season (when mourning expires) there will be a manifestation of God's Word.

Because seeds have reproductive agents that cause them to continuously reproduce after their own kind, the Word that we release in the ears of the hearer will take shape in them; and they will begin to see what you said after a while. Have you ever heard your parents say something that seemingly did not make sense to you, and then you later said, "Oh, now I see what they meant?!" As believers, we don't see with our eyes;

we see through them. Seeing with our eyes limits our reach. Seeing through our eyes allows us to see ourselves as God sees us. Your words have power – God's power. Remember, you're doing the healing through God's Word. They are healed at the point when they receive His Word. It may not look like it: tears may still fall; nights may still be long; graves may still be full. But, the Word of the Lord is eternal, and it will manifest in the season of their lives when nothing is impossible, and everything is available.

www.ingramcontent.com/pod-product-compliance
Lightning Source LLC
Chambersburg PA
CBHW050441010526
44118CB00013B/1622